Water! Water! Water!

written and illustrated by

Nancy Elizabeth Wallace

H₂O
WONDER
EXPERIMENT
OBSERVE
RECORD
YOUNG SCIENTIST SERIES

FUN WATER EXPERIMENTS

FUN
WATER
EXPERIMENTS

two lions

Walter was a warthog who loved water. Walter thought a lot about water in his everyday world.

"Water! Water! Water!" said Walter. "What would we do without water?"

Walter had a new blue notebook.

He started writing about and drawing water.

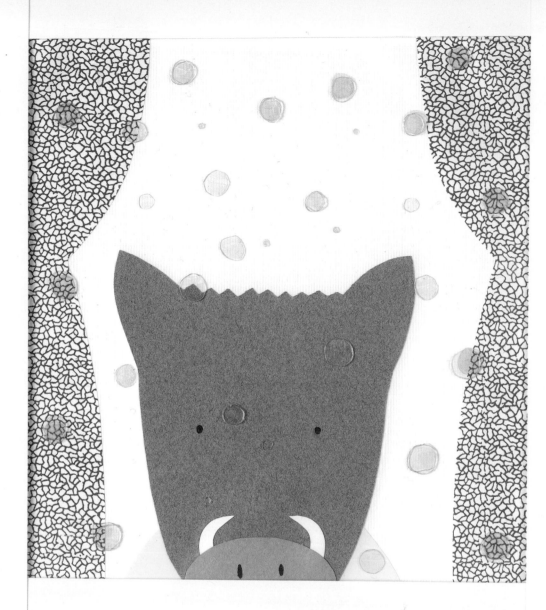

The next morning, Walter spent a long time listening to and watching the rain.
He noticed something he hadn't noticed before. It made him wonder.
   "The raindrops are clinging to the window glass," said Walter.
   "Some drops are small and some are big." He wondered about that too.

So . . .

. . . after breakfast, Walter went to the library.
He borrowed a book.
He read it straight through.

"Water drop, drop, drops,"
said Walter.

"Time to do an experiment."

From the bathroom, Walter got a dropper.

From the kitchen, he got a small bottle cap

and a small bowl with water in it.

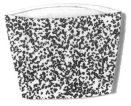

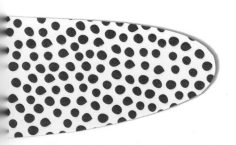

First . . .

. . . he filled the dropper.

Then he gently *squeeeeeezed* the dropper's rubber bulb.

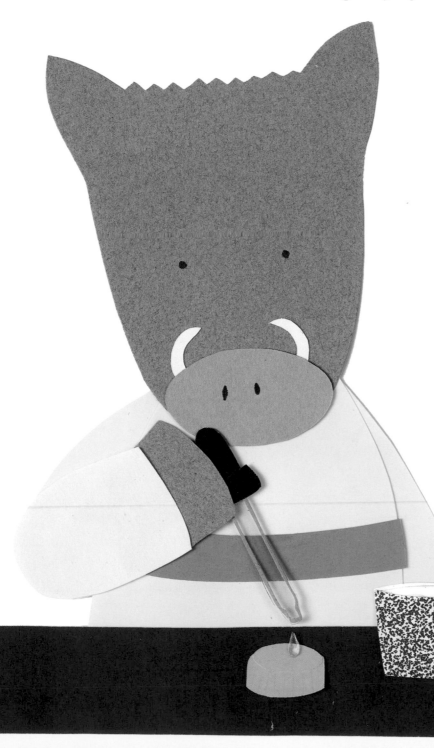

D
r
o
p,

d
r
o
p,

d
r
o
p.

He noticed that when a drop landed close enough to another drop, they pulled toward each other and made a bigger drop. "Wow!" said Walter. "Water drops stick together!"

Walter kept filling and squeezing.
Drop, drop, drop on the top of the cap.

He filled and squeezed. Drop, drop, drop.
The water bulged above the cap.

"Wow!" said Walter.
He added more and more drops . . .

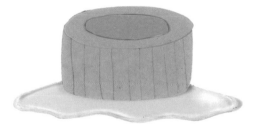

. . . until the bulge got so big that all the drops couldn't
hold together and water spilled off the cap.

He did the experiment again and again. Sometimes
he counted the number of drops. Sometimes he forgot
to count them because he was having so much fun.

Walter wrote about and drew the experiment
in his book.   When he was done . . .

. . . he looked out the window.
The rain had stopped. The sun
had come out.

Walter noticed something on
the pavement.
"Puddles!" said Walter. "I can
do another experiment!"

He got a box of chalk from his art box.

Then . . .

Walter went outside. He drew around a puddle on the patio.

Then Walter went for a walk.

When he got back, he drew a smaller circle around the puddle.

Before lunch, he drew
an even smaller circle around
the puddle.

After lunch, he looked.
"Aha!" said Walter. "The
puddle is gone."
The water had evaporated
into the air.
"More water observations to
add to my book."

Walter went inside.

He noticed that the plant on the windowsill had wilted.

He watered it.
He read a book
while he waited.

He checked the plant.
Walter had a snack and played a game while he waited some more.
He checked again. The water in the soil had been sucked up
       into the roots,
          into the stem,
             into the leaves.

"WOW!" said Walter. "Wonderful water un-wilted you! That goes in my book."

Walter paused. He thought, *My book. Wonderful Water*.

He paused again.

"*Walter's WONDERFUL Water Book*." He smiled.

Then Walter wondered about water traveling up the plant.

"What experiment can I do next?" he said. "I know!"

Walter went to the kitchen. He cut a skinny strip of paper towel with scissors.

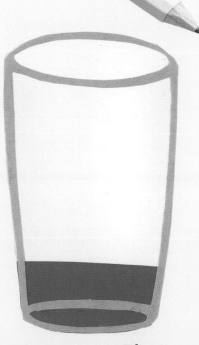

He got a pencil.

Food Coloring

He got a glass, poured a little water into it, and added a few drops of food coloring.

Then . . .

Walter wrapped one end of the paper towel around the pencil.

He set the pencil across the top of the glass so that the other end of the paper towel just touched the water.

Walter watched.

"YES! The water is climbing! It's traveling up the paper towel just like it traveled up my thirsty plant!"

"Now I'm thirsty too," said Walter. "I will get a nice cold drink of . . . what else? Water!"

Walter let the water run for a while to get it cold, but it was not quite cold enough.

He got some ice from the freezer.

He noticed something he hadn't noticed before.

"WOW!" said Walter. "Ice floats!"

After Walter drank the water, he remembered another experiment.

Walter got his mittens from the winter-clothes box in the hall closet.

He got two more ice cubes.

Then . . .

. . . he put on his mittens, picked up the ice cubes, and pressed them together as hard as he could.

He counted to thirty-three.

The ice cubes stuck together.
  "So cool."
  Walter laughed.

"Water can climb, ice can float, ice cubes can stick together. I will add all this to my *Walter's WONDERFUL Water Book*."

So he did.

That night Walter dreamed about water.
"Aaaah," he said in his dream. "Water music."

When Walter woke up, he drew a picture of the dream in his book.

While he was drawing he thought, *Wouldn't it be wonderful to share what I am learning about water with my friend Willa?*

So . . .

. . . he called her.

"Hi, Willa. I'm working on my *Walter's WONDERFUL Water Book*. Want to come over on Wednesday for lunch? We can share some things about water."

"Water?" said Willa.
"On Wednesday?" said Willa.
"What time?"
"One," said Walter.
"Oh," said Willa. "Okay."

After she hung up, Willa
said, "Water, water, water.
What can I share about water?"
Willa really wanted to help
Walter with his wonderful water book.
"I'd better find out more about
water!" she said.

So . . .

. . . Willa got to work.

Planet EARTH

Water

SNOW

H_2O

WEATHER

On Wednesday at one o'clock, Willa showed up at Walter's house.

Walter and Willa had lunch. "Delicious!" said Willa.

After lunch Walter showed Willa what he had written and drawn in *Walter's WONDERFUL Water Book*.

"WOW, Walter!" said Willa.

Then she said, "Thank you for asking me to help you with the wonderful water book."

Walter paused.

"Ask you?" said Walter.

"To help me?" said Walter.

"With *my* wonderful water book?"

Then Willa said, "You know water can be solid."

"Yes," said Walter. "I know that."

"You know water can be liquid," said Willa.

"YES," said Walter. "I know *that* too."

"You know water can evaporate and be gas in the air," said Willa.
"**YES!!**" said Walter.

"But!!! Did you know in nature, on planet Earth, only water can be solid, liquid, and gas?"

"No," said Walter.

"I hope you put that in your wonderful water book," said Willa.

"I will," said Walter. "Thank you, Willa."

"You're welcome. And . . ." said Willa. She reached into her big bag.

She unrolled one
of her drawings.

"Did you know
that most of the
world's water is salt
water, because it's in
the ocean?"

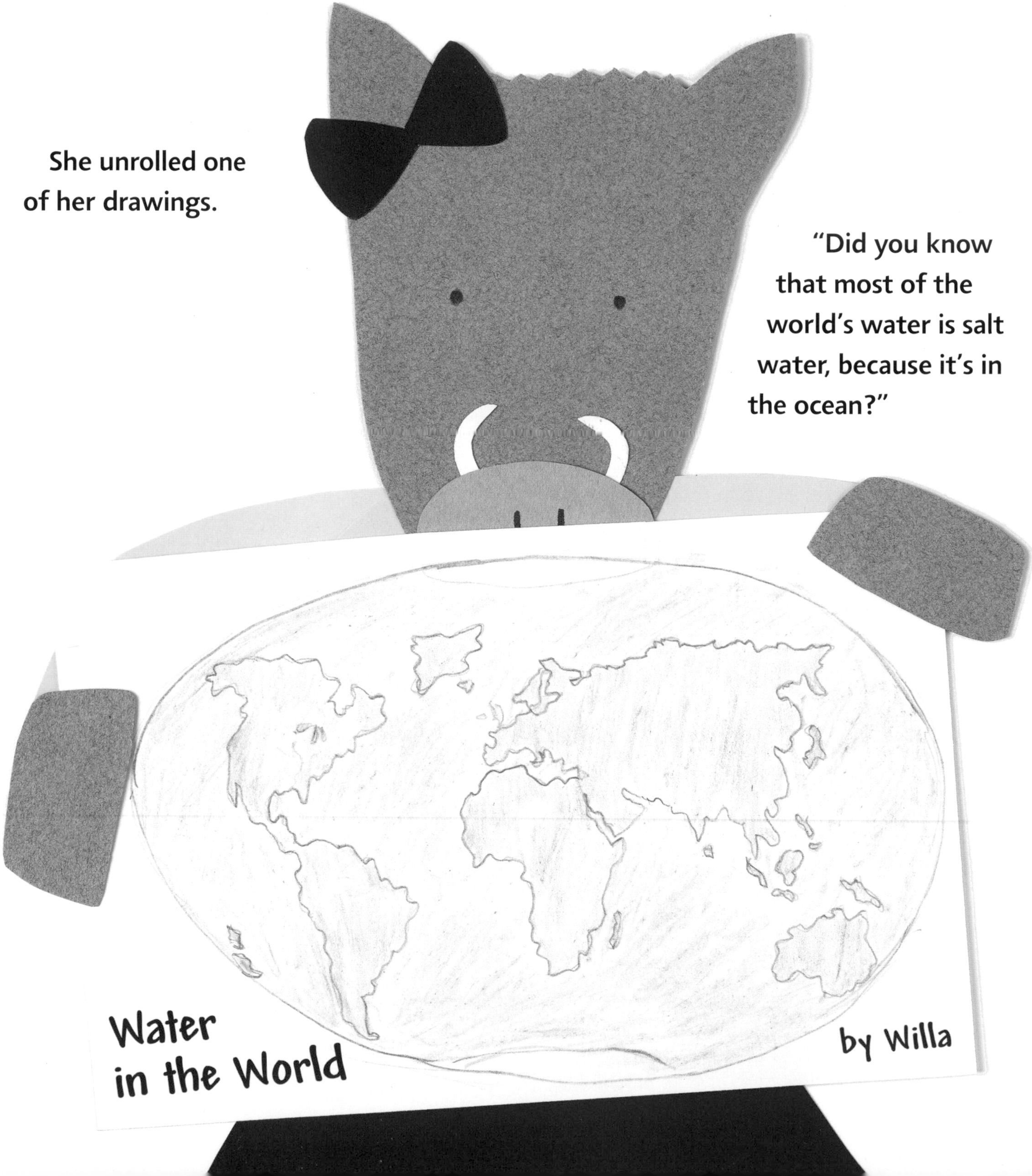

Water
in the World

by Willa

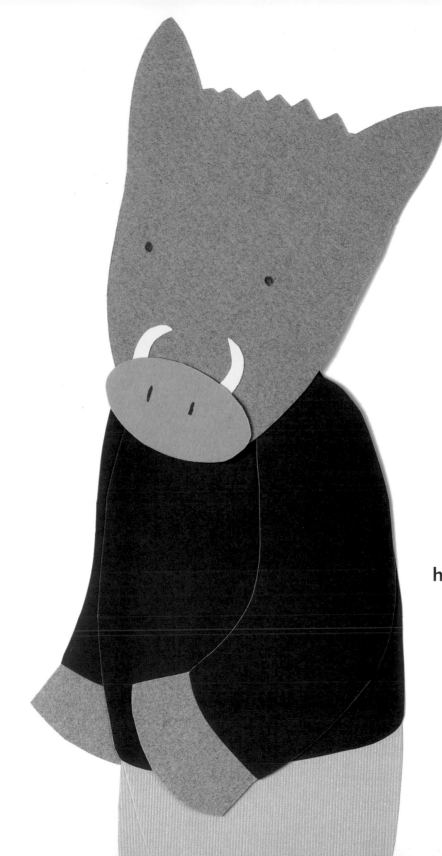

"No," said Walter.

Willa reached into
her bag again.

"Watch! Let's pretend my drawings show all the water in the world.

This little tiny bit is fresh water!

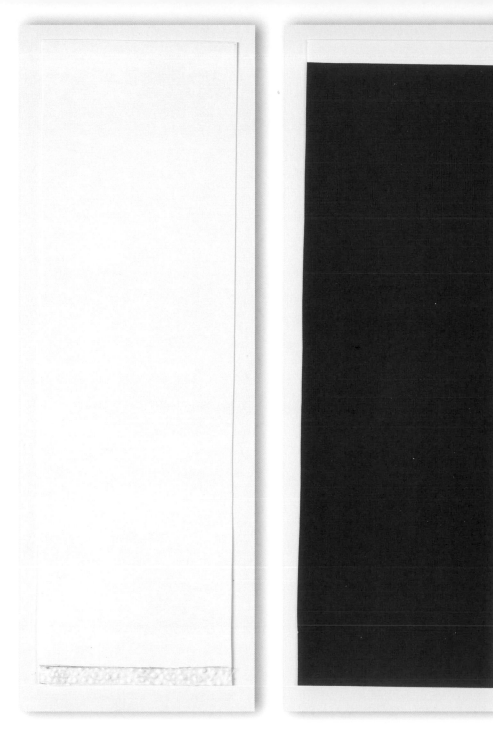

"Oooooh," said Walter worriedly. "I see, Willa!!! I see that there is mostly salt water in the world!"

"Yes," said Willa. "And . . .

This little tiny bit more is snow or ice, so it's frozen water.

This much is salt water!"

". . . did you know that not everyone has enough clean fresh water to drink and cook with and bathe in and water their gardens with and brush their teeth with and wash their laundry with and . . ."

"Nooooooo," said Walter, "I didn't know. Oh, Willa, we must not waste WONDERFUL water."

So . . .

. . . they spent a week thinking of ways they could help save water. They made a list:

Ways Not to Waste Wonderful Water

Take shorter showers.

If you take a bath, don't fill the tub to the top.

Turn the water off when you are brushing your teeth.

If you don't finish drinking a glass of water, use it to water plants.

Have a bottle of cold water in the refrigerator so you don't have to run the water from the faucet for a cold drink of water.

When you wash your hands, wet them, turn off the water, soap them, rub, count to 30, then turn the water back on to rinse.

Tell others how they can help not waste wonderful water too.

For example: Fix leaky faucets. Run only full loads of wash. And keep thinking of more ways to not waste WONDERFUL WATER!

Ocean Blue

Fire Engine Red

And then they put all this and more in . . .

. . . *Walter and Willa's WONDERFUL Water Book.*

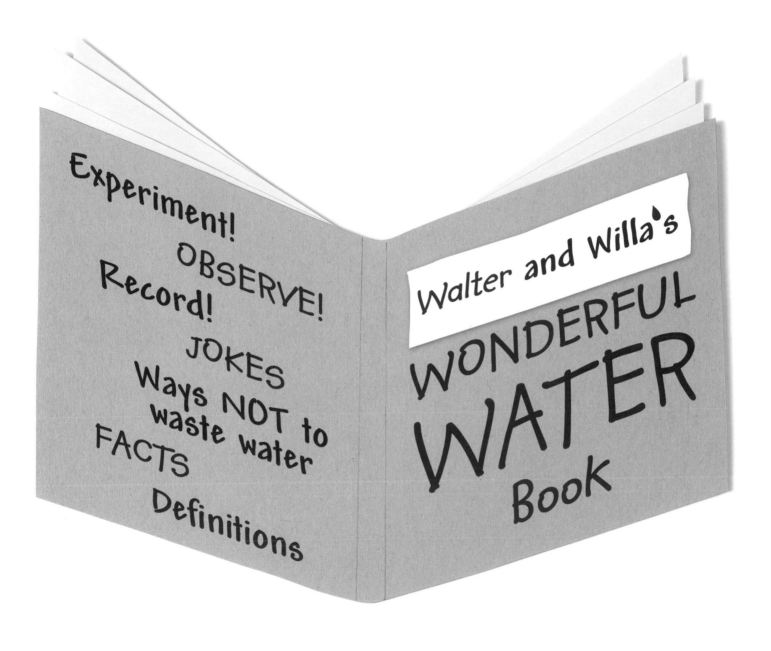

Experiment!

OBSERVE!

Record!

JOKES

Ways NOT to waste water

FACTS

Definitions

Walter and Willa's

WONDERFUL

WATER

Book

Water or H₂O is made of two hydrogen molecules and one oxygen molecule.

You can't see molecules because they are toooooo small!

Joke: Why did Willa throw a bucket of water out the window?

Answer: She wanted to see the waterfall! Ha ha ha.

Evaporation:

When water changes from a liquid or solid to a gas; also called vapor. It seems to disappear!

Surface tension:

When the water molecules that are on top of a drop or puddle or glass of water pull together like a thin skin.

Joke: What can run but never walks?

Answer: Water! Ha ha.

Fire Engine Red

Adhesion: When water molecules stick to other things like window glass.

Capillary action: When water climbs up the sides of a plant's capillaries, which are like teeny tubes inside the plant, because of adhesion. The water level then climbs up because of cohesion.

Only water on planet Earth can be solid, liquid, and gas!

Solid (ice or snow): the water molecules are moving very slowly.

Liquid: the water molecules are moving!

Gas: the water molecules are moving very, very fast and are far apart from each other.

Cohesion: When water molecules stick to each other.

Joke: When Walter threw his soccer ball into the water, what did it become?

Answer: Wet! Ha ha ha.

For Peter and Mom Alexine, with oceans of love always
—N. E. W.

Special thanks and love overflow to Margery, Walter and Dan, Deb and Kate,
Doe, Judy, Kay, Leslie B., Leslie C., Lorraine, Mary-Kelly, Bina, Debbie, Kate D.,
Kate F., Jen and Lynn, Donna and Jan, Lindsay-Lin, Cyd, and Virginia

two lions

Published by Two Lions, New York

www.apub.com

Amazon, the Amazon logo, and Two Lions are trademarks of Amazon.com, Inc., or its affiliates.

Library of Congress Control Number: 2013922872

ISBN-13: 9781477847305 (hardcover)
ISBN-10: 1477847308 (hardcover)
ISBN-13: 9781477897300 (ebook)
ISBN-10: 1477897305 (ebook)

The illustrations were prepared using origami, original art,
recycled paper, recycled plastic, and markers.
Book design by Virginia Pope
Editor: Margery Cuyler
Printed in China
First edition
10 9 8 7 6 5 4 3 2